Concerned Attentions

Knute Skinner

salmonpoetry

Published in 2013 by
Salmon Poetry
Cliffs of Moher, County Clare, Ireland
Website: www.salmonpoetry.com
Email: info@salmonpoetry.com

ISBN 978-1-908836-60-1

COVER ARTWORK: *"The Artist's Studio"* — *photograph by Diarmuid Twohig*
COVER DESIGN & TYPESETTING: *Siobhán Hutson*

Printed in Ireland by Sprint Print

Salmon Poetry gratefully acknowledges the support of The Arts Council.

for Edna

Acknowledgements

Some of these poems have previously appeared (sometimes in earlier versions) in the following periodicals: *Acumen, Agni, Alaska Quarterly Review, Ambit, Blackbird, The Blue Max Review, Books Ireland, The Christian Science Monitor, The Clare Champion, Crannóg, Cyphers, Epoch, Grain Magazine, Grasslimb, New Ohio Review, North American Review, The Poetry Bus, Poetry East, Poetry Ireland Review, Prism International, Quadrant Magazine, Revival Literary Journal, Revival Poetry Journal, The SHOp, The Silt Reader, Skylight 47, Smiths Knoll, Southword, The Stinging Fly, The Stony Thursday Book, Westerly, The Windsor Review*, and *The Yale Review*.

"Dog in the Road" appeared in *Dogs Singing, A Tribute Anthology*, edited by Jessie Lendennie, Salmon Poetry, 2010.

"Ringing the Number" appeared in *Best Irish Poetry in English 2010*, edited by Matthew Sweeney, SOUTHWORD editions, 2010.

"Let Us Know" was broadcast on *The Midnight Muse, Singing Poems from Alaska Quarterly Review*, in a musical setting composed and sung by Amy Lou Hettinger.

"My Cat" and "Me and My Big Sister" were written in response to "The cat removes all doubt" and "Just before sundown"—acrylic paintings by Sara Foust.

Contents

III. *Meetings and Partings*

I.

Concerned Attentions

Green Light

The light changed to green, but his car
remained as it was, at ease,
its engine quietly running,
exhaust making its exit.

The cars that stopped behind him
were anything but quiet.
Their horns, first one, then several,
expressed their dismay.

He can still remember those horns.
They became more insistent, then stopped
once a face, and then other faces,
appeared at the window.

But the memory is fading now.
He barely recalls the opening of the door,
the awkward turn of the key,
the concerned attentions they gave him.

The Holy Well

for Fr Denis Crosby

Michael Healy's Field
St Flannan's Day, 2010

We gather where they gathered before.
Men, women and children of Killaspuglonane,
through years beyond memory,
traversed fields and boreens
to stand where we now stand.
They walked the circular path
that we have walked,
in homage to a sacred place.

May they be with us today
as we meet in renewal,
adding our veneration to theirs.
And may others in years to come
stand where we now stand
and walk the same circular path.
And may the spirit of this well
bless us and those who will follow.

In a Restaurant in Nova Gorica

Slovenia, April 2012

She's chosen her jumper well,
black, a dramatic contrast to her hair—
long and ropey blonde hair,
dyed (though you'd look hard to notice),
the strands falling randomly down from her neck
to lie vivid against her jet-black top.

I hope she's a good friend.
I hope the young man she faces,
looking up now and then from his pasta,
thinks her face, which I cannot see,
compensation for however much of his life
has been in her service.

I hope he envisions her hair as it soon may be,
beneath her, spread out on her pillow,
framing a face that confronts him only with love.

At Gate No. 7 of the Airport at Trieste

(Ryanair-ese for Ronchi del Legionnaire)
26 April 2012

If this low-fares, on-time aircraft should decide
to make an untoward descent,
will these be the chosen ones to accompany me
into the White World?

Flight 169 (God and Ryanair willing) will be boarding soon,
and if so the American woman whose withers
stretch tight the back of her Clearwater Beach jacket
will be one of us.

And so will the young Italian with the half-shaved head,
and so will his wife or lover—with her tower of thick black curls
and her black eyes busy assessing other men.

And so too will the jittery wench positioned
at the head of Ryanair's non-Priority line
(who shifts her weight from one Nike to the other
while trying to adjust a tight-fitting pair of jeans).

The three Irish teenage girls will not be spared,
as their too obvious boredom provides
not a tittle of protection.

The late arrival—out of breath but still half running
while the strap of his cabin bag
(10-kilogram maximum)
digs into his shoulder—
will come to regret haling his heart to this gate.

Edna, the love of my current incarnation,
sits here beside me.
And should it indeed happen
that we share an unscheduled descent,
then together we'll tender ourselves to the Spirit of Light.

And it may or may not come to pass
(but I hope that it will)
that we will once again encounter each other,
the next time around here on the Planet Earth.

A Useful Bench

for Michael Young and Martin Heffernan

We are sitting on a useful bench
placed in memory of someone whose name and dates
are nestled against our backs.
Before us, there are ducks on the pond,
and frustrated dogs in the company of old men
pass up and down the footpath.
An occasional pram, its occupant partially obscured,
is pushed along by a bored-looking parent or two
as it rolls dutifully past us.

In one direction the footpath
meanders uphill to a gateway
which faces Dartmouth Park Hill.
It's the way that we will be going.

At that exit we'll turn to the left,
and at Highgate Hill we will come across cars and buses
jamming their lanes as they inch along,
intent on their destinations.

Then we will proceed to the heart of Highgate Village
and our own destinations.
It is there we will browse in the Highgate Bookshop,
look for a bargain in a second-hand charity shop,
and then (before we return to our gracious hosts
at 83 Dartmouth Park Hill)
enjoy a pint of bitter at The Prince of Wales.

But now, for the moment, it seems to us quite enough
just to sit on this useful bench.
The person in whose memory it exists
will not be going anywhere very soon,
and why should we be in a hurry?

Windows

Celebrate if you wish to
the view from *your* kitchen window,
a stretch of meadow perhaps
with people close to the earth,
backs bent, gathering grass
or loading produce on carts.

Or, it may be, people in gear,
their heads held high, on horseback,
prepared for the chase.

Or, if nothing like that, a high hill
sporting a ruined castle
(or perhaps an aesthetic cottage)
and topped with incomparable trees
that patrol your skyline.

As for me, I like our own view,
the window itself half concealed
by the colander next to the sink,
its dark-green handle pointing
(as if with intent) to the ceiling,

and by the plump cooking pot
half obscuring the top of the blender,

and by the checkered blind
pulled half way down to the sill
on which stands a pot of fresh basil
growing just for us.

And what can be seen *through* this window?
A thorn tree in full, white-bright blossom
that allows (just barely) small spots,
here and there, of a lucent
and confident blue-white sky.

Use

"...as much use
as a second moon...."
Penelope Shuttle

In the beginning, we were made glad
by the new luminosity,
by fewer oppressive nights.

If a cloud degraded one,
we could turn to the other.

Out for a late night walk,
we had one both coming and going,
and if the first was a sliver,
the other approached fullness.

We did not question at first
why it should be this way,
how the sky could be so altered.

All too soon, of course,
we had to deal with the tides.

Rain Today

There's rain today—
look on the bright side:
we won't need to water the garden.

There's rain today
and a lot of it
and wind teasing petals from poppies.

What were our sanguine plans?
Cleaning out the garage
and a trip to the dump.

Would I ever have thought
in my vaulting, insatiate days
I'd miss a trip to the dump?

From Inside the Window

The window looks down upon
the formal garden.

The garden walls itself off
from the climbing meadow.

The meadow comes to a halt
at the lowering sky.

The sky confirms the report
of approaching weather.

The weather will wear itself out
besetting the window.

* *lowering:* the intended word is the one
  that rhymes with *flowering.*

Self-Assessment at Eighty

(After reading Peter Ackroyd's *Shakespeare: the Biography*)

I spend the morning writing a poem. Perhaps it will go into
        a book. My latest, *Fifty Years: Poems 1957-2007*,
        has had welcome reviews.

In the afternoon I file my statements from Fiserv.
        My investments from retirement income are doing
        all right.

Shakespeare, in the closing years of his life, at the height of
        his fame, was semi-retired from the theatre but writing
        King Lear.

He had purchased New Place and had recently invested in tithes.

He was wealthier, by the standards of his day, than I am now.

His achievements, then as now, were beyond compare.

My advantage is that I am still above ground.

The Cat in the Adage

"Letting 'I dare not' wait upon 'I would',
 Like the poor cat i'th'adage"
  —*Macbeth* Act 1 Scene 7

"The cat would eat fish but she will not wet her feet"
  —footnote in *The RSC Shakespeare: Complete Works*,
  Jonathan Bate and Eric Rasmussen, eds.

A kitten, I chased
after anything that moved.
A feather or a teasing finger,
it made no difference.
Flies would come later, then mice.

A cat, I was content
in myself, with nothing to answer for,
responding only when it suited me
to rubbing behind my ears
or a lap to lie on.

In time, sleep would steal on me,
or else long, drowsy minutes
of yawning and stretching
and then yawning again—
before going back to sleep.

And now an old, old cat,
I learn that I'm in an adage.
But Lady Macbeth got it wrong.
Whatever she meant me to signify,
I never lacked for fish.

The Power of Prayer

He braced himself and murmured a prayer.
He could hear himself laughing.
Then "Hey, you," he said, "whatcha doing?"

"I'm praying," he answered, "I'm
just bracing myself and murmuring a prayer."
Then "What's it to *you*?" he added.

They could have gone on like that, he and he,
but the driving rain abated
and an oncoming car swerved clear.

"Well, what do you know!" he said,
and "What do you make of that!" he said,
and "I think I've converted myself,"
they said together.

In the Škocjan Caves

Divača, Slovenia

A drop of water.
On what's left of my nose.
In time I'll be a stalagmite.

Voices above me—
faint, then loud, then faint—
move up and down
slippery footpaths.

Some whisper. Some joke. Some laugh.
As I did.
Some grip the iron railings.
As I failed to do.

The tour guide will shut off the lights.
I'll be left again with the flowing Reka
and the small, blind movements
of salamanders.

The day that voices fail
to come back again,
I'll forget to remember myself.

By that time—it may be—
I will cease to care.

Let Us Know

Let us know how it goes.
That hill looks calm tonight
where the new moon barely shows.

You move on sportive toes
and laugh in the evening light.
Let us know how it goes.

The high horizon glows
in fading Fahrenheit
where the new moon barely shows

and the path obligingly goes,
whetting your appetite.
Let us know how it goes.

God alone only knows
—and even God, not quite—
where the new moon barely shows,

but you, a stranger to woes,
would haste to impending height.
Let us know how it goes
where the new moon barely shows.

In Tourist Season

(before the smoking ban)

for Tom Frawley

The man in the kelly-green pants
asks for a gin and tonic
and settles his bright green arse on a bar stool.
He leans his craft-shop shillelagh against the counter
and, taking out his cigarette lighter,
surveys the shelves of carefully lined-up bottles.

The gentlemanly, elderly barman,
accustomed as he is to all comers,
places a bottle of tonic in front of the man
and beside it a glass with its hand-poured measure of gin.
Then he adopts a stance friendly but distant.

But this narrative does not end here,
for the man on the bar stool asks for ice,
which the bar does not furnish,
and the man on the bar stool asks for lemon;
the result is the same.
"I see," he says, as if he were talking to himself,
though all four walls of the bar can hear him,
"I must lower my expectations."

The elderly, gentlemanly barman,
lifting a cloth from the sink behind the counter,
informs him politely that up the street
he'll find the pubs more upmarket.
Then, using the cloth, he carefully wipes
his visitor's ash from the counter.

Variations on a Line of Verse by Jo Slade

for Edna

Waiting is the possibility of something.
I'm waiting for the sun to set,
and I'm waiting for the sun to rise.
Both things are possible.
I'm waiting for better weather.
That too.

Waiting is the possibility of something.
But is anyone waiting for a banker
to say, "I'm sorry"?
Is anyone waiting for the government
to embrace the poor?

Waiting is the possibility of something.
I'll wait with you at the bus stop.
I'll wait with you for the paint to dry.
I'll wait with you at the checkout counter.

If you were not here, Love,
I'd wait for you always.

My Cat

My cat
isn't like your cat
or any other cat I know.

He won't sit on your lap
or on anyone else's
and purr.

He's not going to lie on his back
and twist one way or the other
and look cute.

He may seem harmless enough
as he turns your way,
but watch out, he's ready to spring.

Black, he thinks he's a panther.

Lover

How he loves going there.
The frisky lights, the brisk pavements,
the sharp colours, the bold gestures,
the expressions that inordinately offer
the heady taste of distraction.

★

How he loves going there.
The soft, irregular lines of surpassing meadows,
the casual release of attending stars,
the small talk of men and women
rooted in a sequence of seasons.

★

How he loves going there.
The key fitting the lock, the turn of the handle,
the door opening to a face
framed by a well-ordered room
with sight lines that lead to a pledged passage.

The End of the Road

I walk along the possible road,
one deliberate step ahead of the next.
At the end of the road, it may be,
there'll be sustenance, shelter,
a sensation of sympathetic hands.

How long will it be, a lifetime?
With each deliberate step
my life lengthens.
What, I ask myself, will there be
at the end of the road?

At the end of the road, God knows,
there'll be sustenance, shelter.
At the end of the road, the road
will begin again.

Hope for Us All

"I'm sick of my life,"
said the new devotee,
slack with submission.

"Don't worry about it,"
spoke the guru, adjusting his robe,
"there's always the next one."

Some Say

There are, some say, lives that we could have led,
choices we could have made, a castle in Spain
we could have occupied; we could have lain
beside each other in Dylan's big brass bed.

We could have savoured viands unlimited,
depleted cellars stocked with rare champagne,
breathed lungful after lungful of frangipane,
and courted renown on steeds high-spirited.

There'd have been, of course, options other than these,
with stations less extreme, fare less exotic,
routines designed for a normal narrative.

And if people *are* free to pick the lives they please,
with a range of choice from quotidian to quixotic,
we well might have chosen, exactly, the lives we live.

II.

Wind

The Last Bus

The last bus to the city has gone,
the very last bus.
We think about that bus as we walk through the village,
dead leaves scudding across the road.

Soon those of us who remain
will walk past bare-breasted trees
to the third village lamp post and back,
the city a pale recollection.

Soon we'll bundle in anoraks and greatcoats
to negotiate footpaths barely scraped clear
of the drifting snow,
the city a wind's breath away.

When the first hesitant shoots
shine in watery sunlight,
we'll gather in tight hopeful knots
at the village square.

Groups

We stood around in groups,
restricted, apart,
those in each group slyly eyeing
those in the other groups.

Each group had its *raison d'être*,
but within each one there were those
who looked out of place
or, at best, ill at ease.

It wasn't a matter of record
how the groups had been formed.
A few among us, old timers,
averred they had always been there.

Others, though short on detail,
surmised that there was a Golden Age,
a time when there *were* no groups,
or rather, just one large group.

And a woman among us,
one we considered fey,
went so far as to state
that our group should disperse.

We viewed her, as was our wont,
with tolerant good will
and continued to eye, slyly,
those in the other groups.

Hearing the News

We heard it all right,
but we didn't believe it.
When the half naked, snot-nosed child
clutching a limp cat
glared at us with the news,
we walked on by.

Well, what would you have done?
The same as we did, perhaps,
when we came upon three old women
bent into each other in a doorway.
They stopped their sibilant whispers just long enough
for one to straighten her back and blurt it out.

When it did actually happen,
they all—not just the old women and the dirty child
but the rail-thin man in a smeared butcher's apron
and the heavily made-up matron offering cheese—
made a circle of sorts around us
expressing their satisfaction.

No Turning Back

The hedge alongside us ended
at a very high wall.
As the wall was too high to scale,
as the hedge was woven tight,
and as there was no turning back,
we had but one option.

The niggard path that offered itself
was generous only with thistles,
and except where it swerved from brambles,
it closely followed the wall.
The squashed cans and broken bottles,
half hidden on either side,
seemed remnants of another time,
bequeathed to nature by people long since gone.

The wall, we assumed, went somewhere
and so too the path,
but the wall remained very high
while the path grew harder to find,
the thistles more thick.

The Dead About Us

Is it long now?
Not as long as it might be
but long enough.

We have that in mind as we set
our work aside,
telling ourselves that it
can wait for again.

For a time, the restless air
is all that moves us.

And then we begin to notice whatever else.
The dead about us for one thing,
their presence known as the moon falls
across the enclosures
and known again as the stones
begin standing out.

Is it long now?
It's long, no question about it.
Although our work remains,
the dead are very well able
to abide the time.

Wind

Though the day has come for us,
the wind is all that seems real.
And real enough it has been,
blackening leaves and stalks
and scattering petals.

Though we will not revert
to our gardens again,
to us they seem infinitely sad
and replete with nondescript meanings.

Arrangements have been made for us,
and as we lack cause for further delay,
we step out into the wind.
We care so little for the future of our past
that we leave our doors open
to swing on their hinges.

Bent forward, we lean on the wind,
assured of each other's presence—
even though our eyes, downcast,
extend no farther than our feet.

III.

Meetings and Partings

Another Headache

I was getting another of his headaches.
There I was, preparing for a good-enough day,
when it made its quiet appearance,
showing itself only in a forced smile
as he walked back into the house after checking the tyres.

But I didn't get it at first.
It was only the averted eyes and the soundless sigh
as he picked up the picnic basket
and then as I marshalled the kids
that told the whole story.

But true to form, when I asked him,
"It's nothing," he said,
making sure that it would be,
for the rest of the long day,
something indeed.

Before and Behind Us

Traffic was backed up.
"It looks like we're stuck here," I said,
touching Marie on the thigh.
I risked a small smile,
which she didn't notice.

Traffic was backed up before and behind us,
but squad cars arrived from everywhere all at once,
their sirens pointlessly wailing.
Their jerky lights splashed colour all over
the line of Marie's tense profile.
Leaning toward her, I kissed her cheek.
"This time at least," I said,
"you'll have an excuse."

Men up ahead moved back and forth,
and someone was being handled
onto a stretcher.
There was blood, perhaps.

A Coat, a Scarf and a Purse

I can see she remembers me,
but I don't think she knows where she's seen me.
She is wearing the same dark brown coat,
with the same yellow scarf wound tight around her neck,
and she's carrying the same red fake-leather purse.
She looks lost and forlorn, but she also looks
much prettier than she has a right to be.

It's clear she doesn't know what she should do.
Should she smile, nod her head, or just walk on?
How awkward she must be feeling.

I could make a decision for her.
I could walk on without a word
about standing behind her a week ago
in the post office queue.
Or I could pause, leaving it up to her
to recall, if she can, just who I may be.

I could also say, "Hello, it's been a long time,
but it's good to see you again."
I could sweep her into a quick embrace
and suggest we go for a drink.
I could undo her scarf
and help her remove her coat.

Curtain Time

"Places, everyone, places!"
She hoists herself to her feet.
"That's our young director," she thinks,
"trying to act his part."

She looks down at the make-up
she's spilled across the floor,
foundation, highlight and shadow
all looking for new places.
She tries not to weep.

Then her eyes move across the room.
"Oh, God," she thinks, "there's Jimmy.
Have they sent *him* to fetch me?
Jimmy, who has a walk-on part?
Jimmy, the age of my son?"

The bit player Jimmy just stares.
"I should help her," he thinks.
"I should ease her into her chair.
I should pick up her make-up."

"She'll have to do it again," he thinks,
"her cheeks are so smeared."

They both hear the knock on the door.
"It's too late for any of that," he thinks.

"Oh, God, it's curtain time," *she* thinks,
"and Jimmy's still here.
I should never have kissed him last night."

And then she takes a deep breath.
"Get a grip on yourself, old girl," she says.
"It's time for your cue."

A Decent Skin

"Oh *him*," she laughed, "he's a decent
skin, I suppose."

She spoke as we left the party,
referring to one of the men
who had clustered around her.

I didn't think much about it
as I drove her back to her house
and followed her into her kitchen
and then up to her bed.

But I do think about it now.

I think of his decent skin as he moves his hands
and then as his groin stretches
and then as he eases his stomach
on top of hers.

Dinner

At once Mrs Johnson stops laughing,
but the children continue, as children will.
"Hush now, your mother is tired," I say,
picking up my cue.
They are instantly stilled.
Then I usher them both to the door
where I tell them to go outside
and play for a while.

Back in the room, I at once remove her tray
and begin to straighten her pillows
and fuss with the bedclothes.
Contempt gathers in her necessary smile.
"You may go now," she says,
"Mr Johnson will want his dinner."

Mr Johnson, of course, will want more than his dinner,
but I go at once to the oven.
The game hens are ready to be served,
as are the baked potatoes and the breaded courgette.
So I stir the soup, fetch the French sticks,
and remove the salad from the fridge.
Then I set our plates and wine glasses on the table.

This job pays well, and I am very hungry
and looking forward to dinner.

Dog in the Road

The dog lies in the middle of the road
indifferent as an occasional car
manoeuvres around it.
Only once, when a driver honks,
does it lift its head from its paws
before settling again on the gravel.
Is this what they have in mind
when they call it a dog's life?

Whatever those words mean,
it's the life I'm living, I suppose,
stuck as I am by this window,
looking out this window at a dog,
at a dog I don't know,
and asking which one of us
will be the first one of us
to get out of the way.

From the Bottom of the Pot

She crushed her cigarette out
and she grabbed her purse,
the colourful, floppy purse I gave her
with the beads and the strips of leather,
and without a see-you-later, my only daughter
marched out the door.
She left me her pale-white aura
and no shortage of second-hand smoke.
I opened the window and then,
as I poured out a cup of coffee
from the bottom of the pot,
the phone started to ring.

And of course it was Mother.
She told me all over again, in added detail,
how no one had shown up yet
to repair the TV;
and all the while she was talking
I read and reread the caption
under a picture of Michelle Obama
in the morning paper.
I'm serving notice that the next time around
I'm looking for better karma.

The Front Door

And when they reached the front door,
we sat very still,
hands gripping hands.
Perhaps they would simply ring the bell,
and perhaps, after a while,
they would leave us alone.

We saw them first in the trees,
eschewing the obvious pathway
which led up to the door.
But even as we fixed our gaze,
they were lost from sight,
swallowed by foliage and mist.
They were, we decided to decide,
a trick of the mind.

And it was only by chance
that one of us looked again.
We were going to open the door, but—
once one of us stopped at the window—
then everything stopped.

And now we are very quiet,
afraid to breathe,
our knuckles turned white.
In a minute or two—
we have to believe it—
they will go away.

The Green Jacket

I stood there holding them in my hand.
"Where did you get those?" he asked,
looking up from the bench where he was closing a vice
on a block of wood.

"In your green jacket," I replied,
standing just at the bottom of the stairs.
"You know the one, the one with a button gone
and a small tear at the elbow—

"the jacket I gave you for Christmas two years ago
after Eddie Bauer put it on sale—

"the jacket you took with you last month
on your fishing trip to Montana."

"Oh, that jacket," he said, and he moved his weight
from one foot to the other.

"I believe these are yours," I said,
and I handed the packet to him
in a way that our hands did not touch.
"Perhaps you have use for them here," I said,
"not just in Montana."

He didn't speak and I turned away.
"I'll go back to my work now," I said
and began ascending the stairs.

"I'm replacing the button," I added,
"and sewing up the elbow."

Her Life Story

She asked to be spanked,
so I did spank her,
but not very hard.

What else did I do?
I listened, off and on, to her life story,
and I used my last condom.

Now she's padding about the room,
looking into my things,
stopping now and again to stand bare-assed
in front of the window.

It's here in the bed somewhere.

She looked better last night at the party
when her vague, evasive words
turned suddenly inside out
and I brought her home.

Does she know I'm awake?
I should say something to her,
offer her toast and coffee,
call her a cab.

Her Sister

She sits down with her sister at the picnic table,
and they make a picture, the two of them,
and I ask myself once again
if I made the right choice.

She's lovely to look at, my wife,
and good with the money,
and good with the kids.
It's seldom she turns away.

I shake off my question and put the ham
on a platter to take to the table.
I can hear the kids at the swings
shouting as if their lungs
were in need of a workout.
They come running at once when I call them,
eager and hungry.

At the table I slice the ham
and can taste already the tender meat
with its crust of brown sugar and mustard.

My wife is radiant, laughing
at another of her sister's jokes,
delivered as usual with her own blend of wry.
The two of them throw back their heads,
and the kids, who don't get the joke,
laugh along with them.

By the time we finish the pie, we've become quiet.
The kids are cranky and tired, and the women
have laughed themselves dry.
The fire is down to embers, and an orange-red sun
is touching the trees at the far end of the park.
It's time now for gathering up.

I have several memories I'd as soon not have,
but there's no way to toss them out with the paper plates.
They'll be with me tomorrow as we wave good-bye at the station,
and they'll hang on for days after.

The Hot Dog

The cab goes off down the street.
They are pleased with themselves,
clutching the satchel between them.
Perhaps they are shaking hands
with the satchel between them.
Perhaps they are even kissing.

I like picturing the two of them
so happy on the back seat.

I cross the street, busy with rush-hour traffic
(I have plenty of time)
and buy a hot dog at a corner stand,
its meat skinny but juicy, on a thick bun
which is pale and insipid.
When I bite, mustard shoots out,
just missing my new sea-green shirt.
The cab is still less than a mile away.
The vender, a squat man with an aproned belly,
laughs as he holds out a paper napkin.
The mustard has landed with a plop
on one of my shoes.

And I laugh too, thinking about the cab
and its progress through dense streets.
I have plenty of time.
What are they thinking of now? How excited are they
by the prospects ahead of them,
so seemingly large?

A Long Good Morning

It was a long good morning
replete with birds in voice at the open window
and with sunshine, each time I turned to him,
full on my back and neck.

And then, when I lay face up,
I saw its radiance in his hair,
framing the look of frenzied excruciation
peculiar to his release.

It had to end of course.
As mornings do, as all of our mornings did.
I sat stroking his leg and looking out
on the view that I had gradually learned to share.

And then we took a shower and we drank some tea.
And then he said a memorably brief good-bye
as he fingered his ticket home.

Mc and My Big Sister

If I hold on tight enough,
I will be all right.
I won't slip off my seat.
I won't fall down
on my dark shadow.

My sister never sees her shadow.

She is up there above me,
high and dreamy.
She doesn't see
the bad sky behind us.

I'm scared for my big sister.

When we get off our swings,
if I take her hand,
if I take her the safe way home,
she will be all right.

The Monkey Puzzle Tree

"I have to take a leak first," he said.
He started to leave her standing there,
but he came right back.
"Would you hold this a minute?" he asked,
and he handed her the monkey puzzle tree.

It was awkward for her to hold
and heavier than it looked.
When she didn't hold it just right,
it scratched her wrist and, worse,
it snagged her clothing.
She was wearing her dark blue suit.

So, setting down the monkey puzzle tree,
she stood guard,
having positioned it next to the wall.

She thought about the day before,
how they argued about her sister all over again,
how they carried home Peking duck
and ate it in total silence,
how, at the same moment in bed,
they turned toward each other.
Then she saw that the store was closing.

After Security came back
from looking in the men's toilet,
she lugged the monkey puzzle tree outside.
Not having her key to the car,
she hailed a cab.
Although she knew that it made no sense,
she hoped she would find him at home
waiting there for her.

Instead, she ate a fried egg on top of
the left-over fried rice.
And later, when she phoned the police,
they told her he hadn't been missing
long enough to be missing.

When the police did arrive, at long last,
to ask for his photo,
the monkey puzzle tree was still in the hall.
She left it there for another week
before giving it to her sister.

Morning and Afternoon

I nodded and followed Granger to the car,
then watched as he clumsily belted himself in
and found the ignition keyhole.
At the last minute I stuck my head through the window
and gave him a kiss on the cheek.
"Don't even think about it," I said.
"I'll be here when you get back."

Whether he thought about it, I can't say.
I thought of nothing else all morning.
I thought about it washing up breakfast plates,
finding his second dirty sock,
hoovering the carpet where we had knocked over
my busy lizzie.

After lunch I propped myself up on the sofa
and re-read the last chapter of a library book,
one where a plucky young wife
makes friends at last with her husband's teenage son.
Granger no doubt would find the novel trashy,
as he does, more or less, every book he reviews
for the Sunday paper.
But it was a distraction.

At four o'clock I made a decision, almost,
staring into the bedroom closet,
deciding which dresses I could do without.
But by five o'clock I was in the kitchen again,
brushing mushrooms and weighing noodles,
opening the stroganoff mix,
uncorking the red wine to let it breathe.

Old Postures

It was no surprise they were there
on the veranda.
At first they had kept themselves
on that stretch of weed-strewn sand
between the dock and the boathouse.
They came always at dusk,
and they stood there as if—as if—
they didn't know I could see them.

Later, some days later,
they appeared at the end of the garden
between the empty fish pond
and the barrel where we once burned trash.
Staring hard, I could make them out
just beyond the apple tree,
assuming and losing shape
in the fading light.

And now here they are at the house,
on the other side of this locked window,
arranged in old postures,
begging, accusing.
They are standing there stock still
while I stand in the dark hall,
Bible in hand.
If I drew the blind, I could see them.

Ringing the Number

Ringing the number,
I let my finger hang in the air.

I think of the one at the other end
of the call I have not yet made.

She is stabbing a cigarette out
and pouring a second or a third cup of tea.

She is slipping out of her faded Chinese robe
and easing a thick leg into sudsy water.

She is painting her nails,
toe after toe in dark scarlet fury.

She is taking her pills, or else
she's neglecting to take them.

And I? I am telling myself
to ring her number.

Routines

This morning he doesn't say it.
Sitting up in bed, a cup of coffee in his hand,
news droning on in the background,
sunlight cast on the wall,
he looks at me as he always does,
but he doesn't say it.

Yawning and stretching, I nevertheless
manage to prepare our breakfast
while he pours out orange juice and feeds the cat.
Then we sit down to eat in the breakfast nook,
the usual ham and eggs and toast
spread out on our plates.
We forget to take the butter out of the fridge,
and as usual it's hard to spread.

On Sunday mornings we linger after we eat,
scanning the lead paragraphs in the papers,
watching birds as they land and take off again.
Then after the washing up we put out the cat,
put on our bicycle helmets and head for the park.

This Sunday we find ourselves
sitting on the same fallen log,
watching the slow passage of the brown water.
"You didn't say it," I say at last,
taking away my hand.
"This morning you didn't say it."

"How could that be," he answers
as his eyes widen,
"when all the time I was thinking it
all the time?"

The Ruins

Two arms slipped around my waist
as I stood there looking at the ruins.

I'd come thousands of miles to see them,
and I wouldn't have felt let down
no matter how long I stood there looking,
taking in the graceful sweep of broken walls,
the warm greys of fallen stones,
the odd presence of a living past.

I had left her, after our quarrel,
at a small table outside a village café
two or three miles from our modest hotel.
I had set off alone, camera in hand.
It was, after all, what I'd come for.

I stood there a long few minutes, rooted,
her arms around me,
confused by the unexpected mix
of vision and touch.
And then I eased her around,
and together, with careful steps,
we passed into the ruins.

I did get a few murky shots
taken later in the gathering dusk,
and I promised myself I'd return the following day.
The next three days, however, came windblown and wet,
and we sat in the forced cheer of the hotel bar.
The day after that the proprietor's talky son
drove us down through the narrow pass
to our scheduled flight.

Seafood

It was in the market I met him—
on my way back, a bottle of wine in my bag,
a baguette under my arm.

I could have missed him entirely.
A turn to the left would have led me
past stalls of fruit—
oranges, pomegranates, grapes, melons, figs—
then onto the narrow passage
pointing me home.

But no, I walked by the seafood
and—before I knew what was coming—
into his arms.

I live with his unblinking eyes,
the odour of drink,
and of course his pathetic story.
I remember too the long tables of seafood—
calamari, bream, shrimp,
grouper, red mullet, hake....

Why did I walk past those stalls?
I've never liked fish.

She's Back

"She's back again?"

"She is," he answered, crossing to the locker
and rummaging for his boots.

"Is she back long then?"

"She is not," he said, sitting down on the kindling box.
"She showed up last night."
He forced the stiff cold boots over swollen feet.

"Is she staying long?"

He walked to the door and looked outside
where clouds separated and merged
in a patchy sky.
The cattle yard was trodden mud, all over and back.
"She says not," he said, and he buttoned up his anorak
and stepped through the doorway.

"She'll be gone soon then?"

He turned on the gravel and looked back
to where I stood, half slumped on the threshold.
I stood there shuddering in the sharp wind
and feeling that wind through my thin bones.
He coughed a minute and he spat
on the wet gravel.
"I don't know," he replied
and then cleared his throat.

"She's back again then," I said.

He swung around, facing the wind, and trudged
the long path to the van.

The Side Altar

I walk over to a side altar.
Temporary scaffolding blocks the view
of a good half of an Annunciation;
as for the rest, the dark pigment
is lost in the dim light.
Even so, I take a seat on the hard bench
as if the scene held some absorbing interest.
I check my watch, and I bide my time.

Behind me, tourists come and go.
Their attentions focus, reasonably, on the Tintoretto,
or else their necks crane to the stained glass.
Their guarded whispers and careful feet attest
to the respect that tourists assume
they should assume.

It's God's joke on me if they are right,
but perhaps they are.
Perhaps some day I will stand
at the foremost altar,
sickened with recollection.

But for now, I'm here as planned,
trying not to look at my watch,
trying not to slip my hand
into my satchel.

Something in the Grass

She is kicking at something in the grass,
grass halfway up to her knees nearly,
knees no doubt as coarse
as her bare elbows.

Add a few years and she is my mother
out in the yard kicking spirits away
as she feeds the chickens.

Passing, I try not to stare,
but I take in a dirty-blonde head
and a worn shirt open at a scrawny neck.

Beyond, I give her the crazed eyes
that dog me from life to life.

Taking Stock

I walk up to the door and knock.
Nobody answers.
I pass through the side garden,
a straggle of sorry roses,
and around to the back entrance.
Again nobody answers.

What does it mean? I ask
as I sit in a wooden lawn chair
and take stock of the day.
The chair has a rough surface
of peeling paint,
and one of its arms is missing.

I look down at my feet,
sore from the four-mile walk
up from the station.
If I set off at once, I just might
make the 6:25.

Or else I can sit here looking at the path
that leads to an overturned barrow
and a ripped-open bag of compost.

I can watch as the weak March sun
slips behind the shed
and shadows stealthily lengthen
on nettles and dock.

Today and Tomorrow

"Is it serious?" I asked.

"They don't know yet," she answered
and stared off into the distance.

My gaze followed hers out her library window
through the thin bare limbs of her sally trees
down a sweep of sun-drenched,
furze-covered hillside
and out to the open sea.

At the edge of land lay a strip of holiday homes,
identical chalets in bright pastels,
empty this time of year.
She had fought them as best she could.

After a moment she stood up,
waving aside my assistance,
and moved toward the fire.
A sudden spatter of raindrops burst on the panes
and as suddenly ceased.

She bent over, tense and wheezing.
I held her as best I could
till her body relaxed.

"Take a look outside and tell me," she said,
straightening and adjusting her robe,
"if you see a rainbow.
I'll be hearing from them tomorrow."

Touching Him

He put his coat back on.
Then he took it off.
He sat down hard on a chair.
Then he stood up and stared out the window.
It looked like there'd be no let up.
In fact it was looking worse.

Nothing I could do would help him,
but I crossed to him anyway
and touched his shoulder.
I can't say he shrugged me off,
but he didn't respond.
All afternoon he'd imagined a life
while he lost himself in my body.
And look where it got him.

"I'll go now," he said at last,
and I helped him into his coat.
"Be careful," I said at the door.
He kissed me good-bye, of course,
but his head was a mile away,
out on the highway.

I watched as he started his car
and then scraped snow from the windows,
his body tense and his mind probably tenser.
A difficult drive would lead to an uncertain welcome.

I watched him once more as they lowered him down
where none of those present could touch him.
Not those close by the graveside, tragic and drained,
and I least of all, on my own,
at the edge of the crowd.

Years Later

He was filling bags of brown rice
when a pale, wispy young woman
opened the door to the co-op.
She stopped just inside the doorway,
her eyes drifting.
"I'm looking for a man," she said.

Unsure just what she meant,
he ventured a joke of sorts.
"Here I am," he replied, "if you don't mind
one or two grey hairs."

And that should have been the end of it
once she answered him back.
Instead she just stood there looking
as if she would wilt.
He left his work behind him
and brought her a chair.

And so now here they are years later.
He's filling bags of brown rice,
and she is aimlessly humming her tune
while she stocks the shelves.

At dinner he will cook his usual dish,
which she will eat as if she had never
seen it before.
Then after they listen to music, they will go up to bed,
to the same bed where he tucked her in
after hanging CLOSED on the window.

KNUTE SKINNER was born in St. Louis, Missouri, but for fifty years has had a home in County Clare, where he now lives with his spouse Edna Faye Kiel. His collected edition *Fifty Years: Poems 1957-2007*, from Salmon, contained new work along with work taken from thirteen previous books. His collection *The Other Shoe* won the 2004-2005 Pavement Saw Chapbook Award. A limited edition of his poems, translated into Italian by Roberto Nassi, was published by Damocle Edizioni, Chioggia, Italy, in 2011. A memoir, *Help Me to a Getaway*, was published by Salmon in March 2010. www.knuteskinner.com